Ponytail

Young Girl

Teddy cuddle

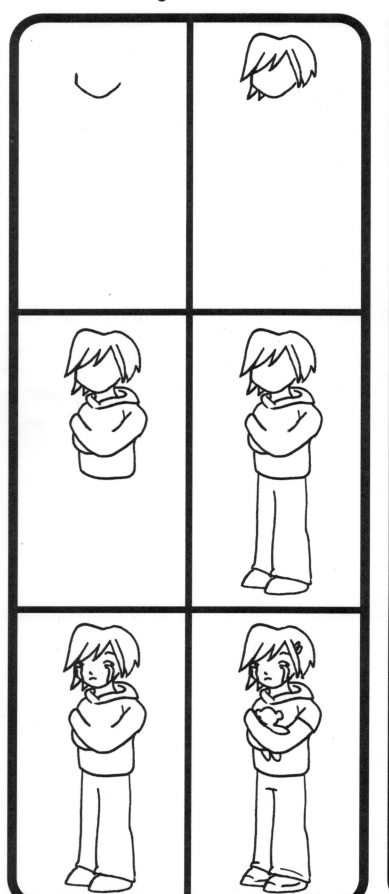

Happy Girl

School Girl

Trendy Girl

catsuit

Skipping

Dancing

Cool Girl

Sleepyhead

curly Hair

Thumbs Up
Annoyed

Laid Back

Shy Girl

Braids

School Boy

Soccer Player

Angry Boy

Grumpy Boy

Relaxed

Trendy Boy

Cool Boy

Smart Boy

Waving

cookies

yo-yo

Attitude   Skater

Shy Boy

Bandana

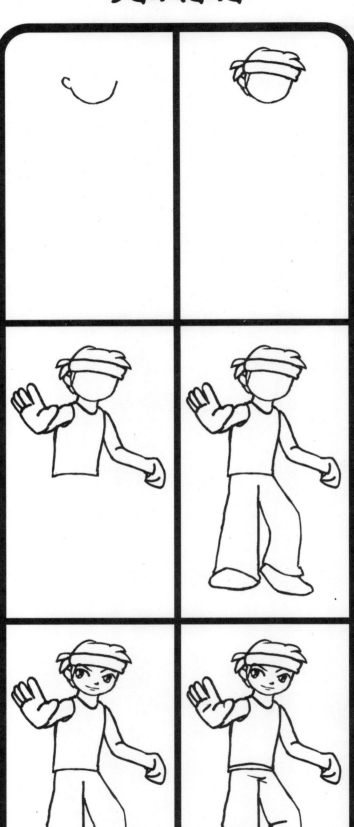

Hoody

Ready to Go

Magical Women

Business Woman

Dancer

Athletic Woman

Racer

Walker

Karate Girl   Japanese Lady

Psychic

Winter Woman

Mother

Archer

Smart Lady

Party Woman

Smart Guy   Relaxed Dude

Karate

Runner

Arms Folded

Elf Archer

Spaceman

Magician

Mystic

Aviator

Rocker

cool Man

Leader

Cool Dude

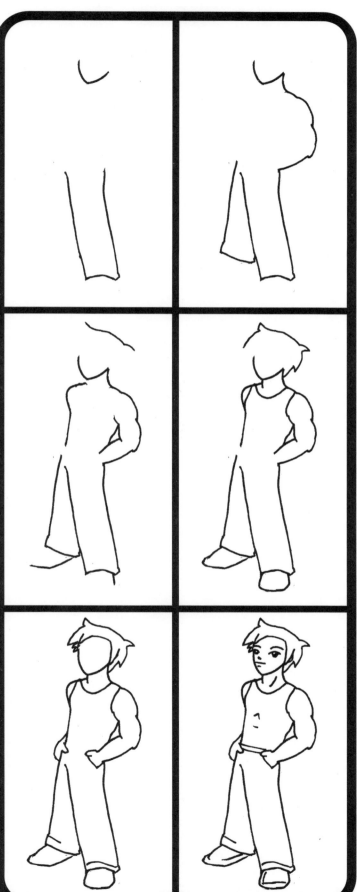

Lamsa

Firefoxy

Shetlan

Springfoot

Anloo

Groob

Bim

Floopsey

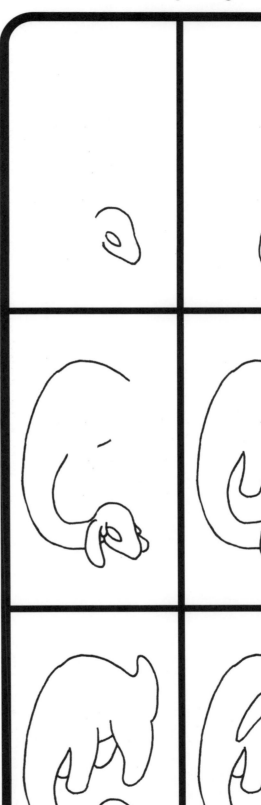

Fire Storm

Mewm

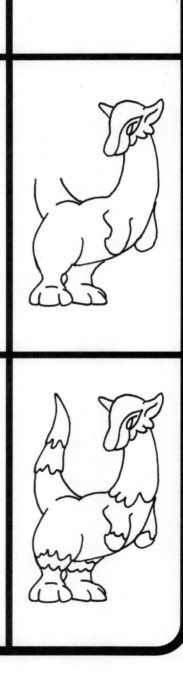

Frosty

Twitch

Anglor   Flambow

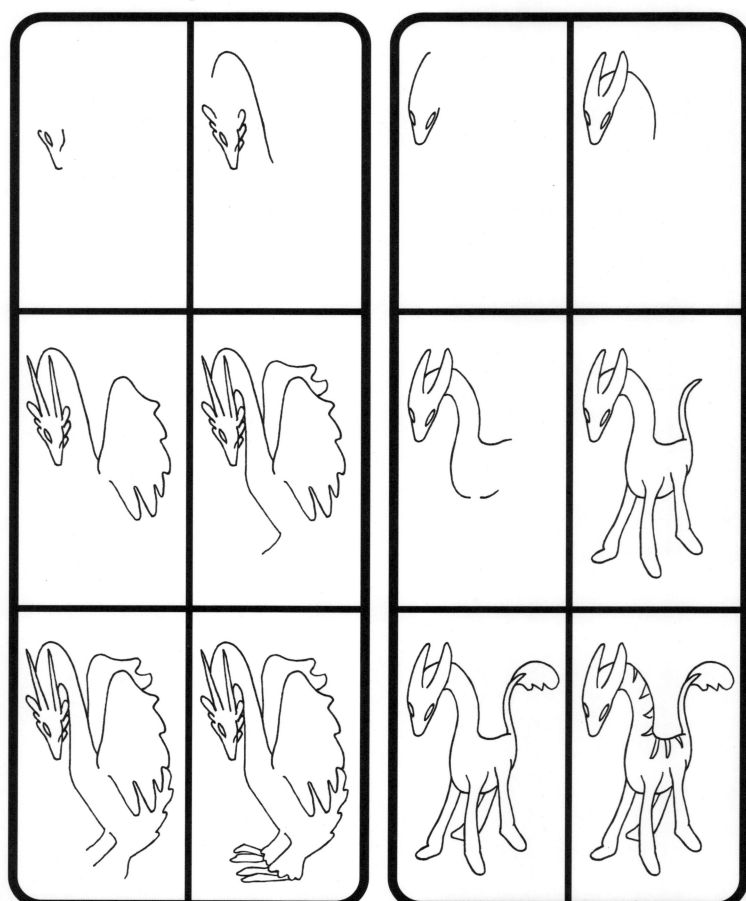

Jelojoup

Brushtail

Robot 1

Robot 2

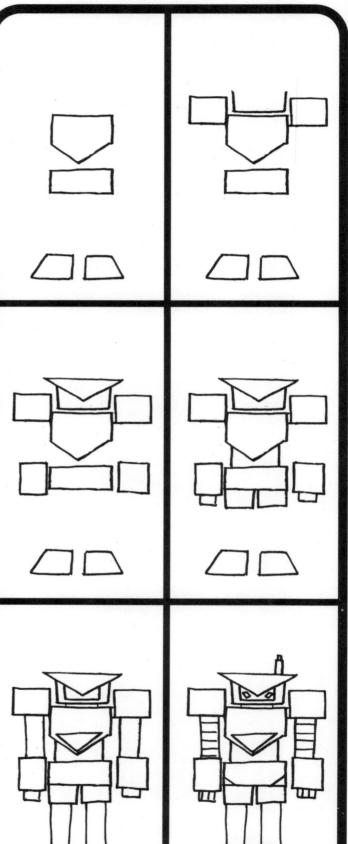

Robot 3 Robot 4

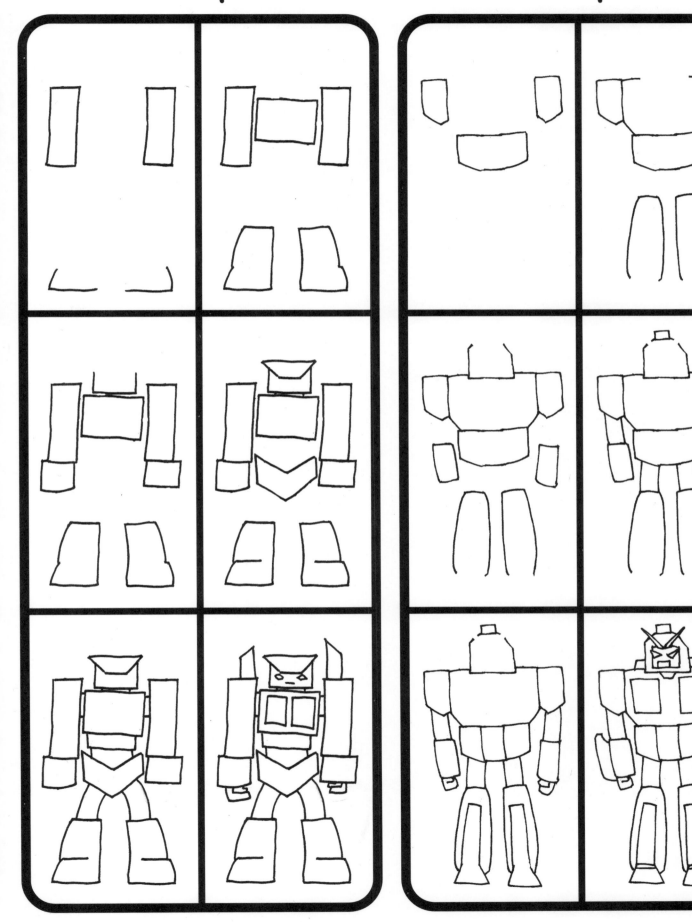

Robot 5

Robot 6

Robot 7

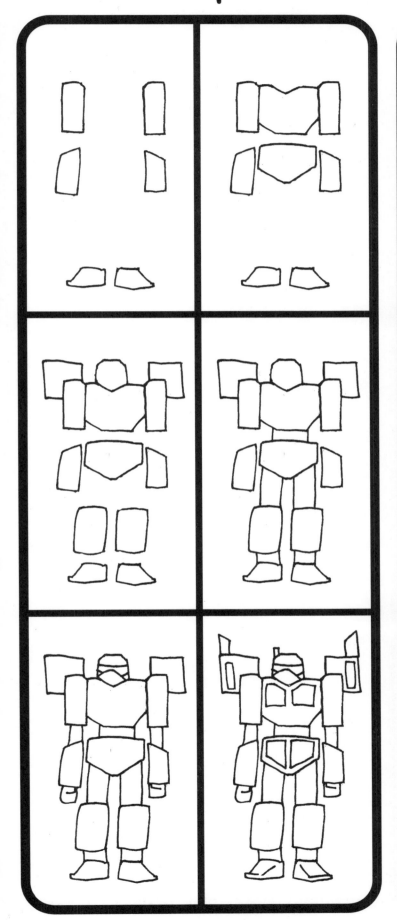

Robot 8

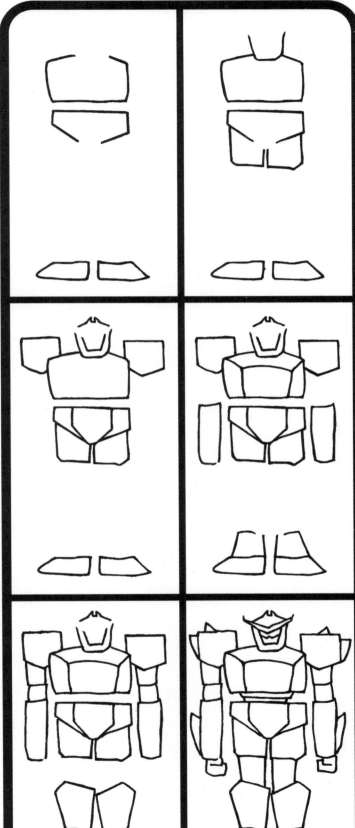

Pleased

Interested

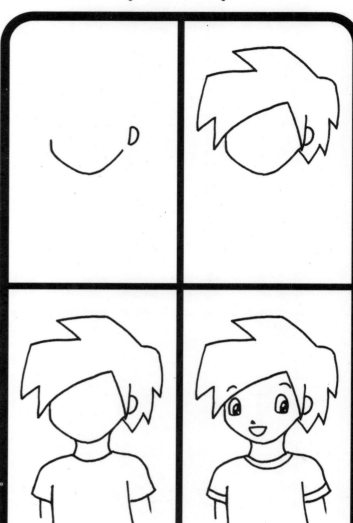

Shy

Happy

Amazed

Worried

cross

crying

Shouting

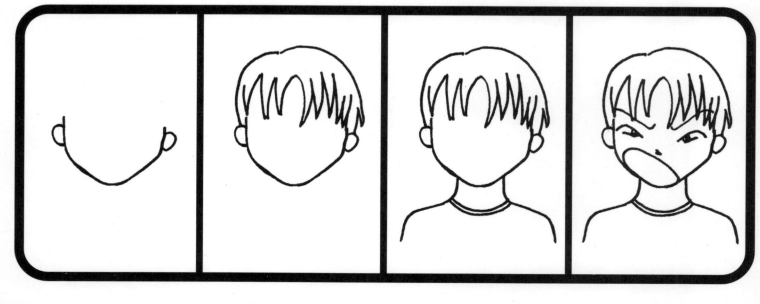

Shock

Wink

Tongue out

Fed Up

Demure

Thinking